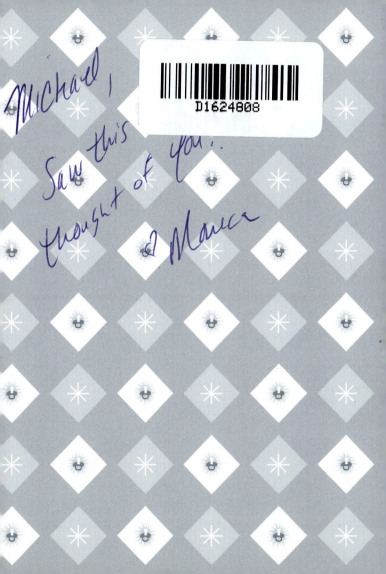

Michael,

Saw this &
thought of you...

♥ Maura

CROUCHING FATHER, HIDDEN TODDLER

CROUCHING FATHER,
HIDDEN TODDLER
A ZEN GUIDE FOR NEW DADS

BY **C. W. NEVIUS**
ILLUSTRATIONS BY **BEEGEE TOLPA**

CHRONICLE BOOKS
SAN FRANCISCO

Text copyright © 2006 by C. W. Nevius.

Illustrations copyright © 2006 by Beegee Tolpa.

All rights reserved. No part of this book may be reproduced in any form without written permission from the publisher.

Library of Congress Cataloging-in-Publication Data available.

ISBN 0-8118-5207-5

Manufactured in China.

Designed by Meghan Eplett

Distributed in Canada by Raincoast Books
9050 Shaughnessy Street
Vancouver, British Columbia V6P 6E5

10 9 8 7 6 5 4 3 2

Chronicle Books LLC
85 Second Street
San Francisco, California 94105

www.chroniclebooks.com

To Mary, who made this possible.
To Will and Molly, who made it necessary.
You are the best parts of my life.
And to my dad, who showed the way.

INTRODUCTION

Remember when you used to go to a restaurant, and some-one's child was fussing and crying, disturbing other diners, and you wondered why in the world the parents didn't do something to take care of the problem?

You know what you should have done in that situation? Gotten their phone number. Because now that you have your own you'll be wanting to call them to apologize. It isn't as easy as it looks.

Not that you will have any second thoughts. Having a kid is going to be great. There aren't many times in your life when you can point to a moment that changes everything forever. This is one. Almost nothing will be as it was. And those things that remain, well, they are transformed too.

You know how you used to walk past a kids' soccer game? Probably held your interest for about thirty seconds, right? What if I told you that in a few years you will likely be on the sideline with your heart pounding, so overwhelmed with emotion you can hardly breathe? Oh, did I mention that the players are just five years old?

You say you don't believe that? Not a problem. I'll give you my phone number. You can call me later to apologize.

This is a book based on real-life experience, but it doesn't pretend to have answers. These entries are more like snap-shots of memories. What works for you may not be what worked for us. In fact, if there is any lesson, that's probably it. The varieties of kids, parents, and the interactions between the two seem almost endless.

And yet, there's a bond that we all understand. Think of it as the space between you and your child when you reach out to give her a hug. Somewhere, in that gap, between coming closer and standing alone, is what being a dad is all about.

Now, a word about Zen. We would like to announce that those responsible for this book have spent decades studying the small nuances of the Zen philosophy.

Unfortunately that's not true. The truth is that the author knows a little about Zen, in the same way that he knows a little about hitting a sand wedge and operating a chain saw. In each case he learned these skills for the same reasons: necessity, opportunity, and fear of embarrassment. Fatherhood, like golf and landscaping, is one of those undertakings in which you muck around on your own until you discover some things that work. Most of the time. (Ask my golf partners.)

But there isn't any doubting that the Zen way makes a lot of sense in these confusing early moments of fatherhood. The idea of *wu wei,* or not pushing and simply letting things happen, rings true. It is a fine concept, and worth striving for. With that in mind I hope that any Zen masters who read this will accept the riffs on the philosophy as they were intended— with humor and goodwill.

In this book you will find suggestions, hints, and nudges. Hopefully you will catch a few smiles, and—if the planets align perfectly—a heartwarming moment of insight or two.

You will not find many rules, although we've had lots of them in our house. Unfortunately, as our first child has pointed out repeatedly, the nonnegotiable edicts we imposed on him turned out to less ironclad when we had a second child. When we gave her a ride to school (he had to walk), or let her stay up until ten o'clock (his bedtime was earlier when he was her age), he would rage at the unfairness of it all. Hey, what can we say? We were new on the job.

It is also hoped that, although this is a book for dads, moms will find something of value in it too. If nothing else it might be a look into the mysterious workings of the "guy mind," a complex, yet oddly primitive, organism.

SAMURAI SLEEPING

When the future White House chief of staff arrives at home from the hospital, you may find he snoozes peacefully during the day (leaving you to watch the NBA Greatest Games on cable TV while eating grilled cheese sandwiches), but when night comes, it's party time! He wants to be held, bounced, and indulged, and, just when your sleepy eyes can't take any more, there is crying.

This points up an important secret that has never been revealed to the public before—babies sleep backwards.

This may be the result of nursing staff schedules. At the hospital during the day, things are so busy that the nurses don't have the time to do much more than check to be sure that the baby is safe and warm. But at night, after visiting hours are over, babies may be picked up, cooed at, and maybe even rocked and snuggled.

If you were a baby, what would you do? Rest during the day and save your energy for those disco nights, of course. For this there is only one cure—samurai sleep training.

Cold, wet napkins should be touched to the baby's cheek and toys rattled when his eyelids start to droop. The idea is to keep him awake as long as possible, hopefully into the evening, when he will crash like a college freshman after midterms.

Be forewarned: for this you may become known as "the Meanest Dad in the World." But when the baby begins to sleep most of the night, you'll happily accept the title.

FINDING YOUR CENTER

How about that baby? Seriously. Incredible, right?

Couldn't you just sit there and watch her scrunch her little face for hours? How about when that tiny hand squeezes your little finger? Is that a miracle of life or what?

So why do you feel an irresistible urge to run out the door? To get in the car and drive somewhere? Anywhere? To go to the office so you could walk over to the coffee machine and ask if anyone saw the game last night?

Admit it. There are moments when, as adorable and wonderful as your baby is, you want to get away. Is there something wrong with you?

Yes. There is. You should seek professional help right away.

Just kidding. Of course not. You've just got the infant-induced version of cabin fever, known as "baby fever." Too confined, too shut in, too many diapers and binkies and jolly little musical bells on the Mr. Jingle play station. You need to step outside and do a little of what the yogis call "finding your center." Take a moment, speak to adults in a normal tone of voice—perhaps operate some power tools.

Do it. You'll feel better.

POOP:
ONE OF THE THREE TREASURES

In general, your baby's job description can be boiled down to three simple tasks—eat, sleep, and poop. You could ask him to clean out the garage, but it isn't likely to happen. Babies have an excellent union.

The eating and sleeping go along pretty much as you might have expected (although not at the hours you had in mind), but the pooping part is a revelation.

Someday, when you arrive home and say to the woman you once kissed passionately and publicly in the doorway of her apartment, "Did we have a good poop today?" all will be clear.

Pooping is many things. It is positive proof that things are running smoothly at both ends of the baby and a surefire deterrent to the dreaded red-faced, tear-streaked, sleep-stealing colic.

But, most of all, it may very well be the first shared positive experience in your new family. Later on in life your child may boot a ball past a soccer goalie or ace a spelling test, but it is entirely possible that the first real praise you give him will be for a timely and productive poop.

Others, baby-less, will wrinkle their nose in disgust, but you will know better. And, as you watch your baby's face, and see a blissful smile creep across it as he completes this task, you will receive a reminder of the joy of the simple and basic.

SATORI:
A MOMENT OF REALIZATION

You're in the car, stopped at the light. An attractive somebody in the crosswalk gives you that look. No, nothing that is going to ruin your marriage. Just one of those fleeting, strangers-on-a-train, eye-contact connections.

You smile. She smiles. There is a moment. And then she laughs. Still nice, but less like flirting and more like she's seen a cute puppy.

What happened? Follow her eyes. There, in the back of the car.

Baby seat.

TEETHING: THE TOOTH OF TIME

It would be a wonderful thing if someone came up with a better method for making baby teeth appear. But so far we are stuck with the time-honored process, which is to let each tooth push slowly through the gums.

This hurts. Complications ensue.

You will hear many suggestions for dealing with the pain of teething. Some will talk of a chilled, soft rubber ring to gnaw on (the baby, not you). Some will even suggest rubbing ice cubes on the gums.

Nonsense. (Picture yourself hanging on to both an ice cube and a baby, and getting them both to cooperate for gum rubbing. Ridiculous.)

What you should do is get to the pharmacy and pick up some teething gel. It comes in small, toothpaste-like tubes. You squeeze a small glob on to your index finger and rub it on the gums. The effect is instantaneous. The crying may stop in mid-wail.

Now, there is no doubt that the Internet was a terrific development and landing on the moon was swell. But the guy who came up with teething gel—now *that* was a scientific breakthrough.

THE UNSTOPPABLE CHI OF DROOL

Baby drool is one of the most persistent and pervasive substances known to science. Drool has a chi, or life force, all its own.

And that's fine. Mostly. When the baby falls asleep on your shoulder and a little milky slobber leaks out of those adorable lips it can be irresistibly cute.

But not on your good jacket. Or your necktie. The only thing worse than noticing at the last second that you are wearing baby drool is *not* noticing and strolling into a big meeting or job interview and having someone point to your shoulder and say, with that pinched, uncomfortable wince, "You've got a little . . . something . . . there."

Unfortunately, we have some bad news. This is going to happen. Baby drool cannot be curtailed, contained, or controlled. It can pass through doors, penetrate plastic, and defy time and space.

But here's the thing. If, for example, you are wearing that dark suit for the big presentation and you have just taken one last look in the mirror to make sure your tie is straight and you look over and see your baby girl reaching her arms up because she wants to be picked up, there is only one thing to do.

Pick her up, for God's sake.

THE EGO MIND AND BABY ENVY

In the beginning you will be delighted with just a smile. That wrinkled, red-faced, tiny little bundle you brought home from the hospital recognizes you! And smiles when he sees you. Incredible.

And then when he learns to roll over, and then sit up, then stand, and begin to walk it is almost too much to believe. How about when he says his first word? And (we don't want to make too much of this, of course) suppose that word is "Da-da"? Let's just admit it: your baby is perfect.

Right up until you go somewhere and meet another baby who's exactly the same age. And that baby already has teeth. And is walking, not crawling. And reads the *Wall Street Journal* every morning.

Don't go there.

Look, this gets worse, not better. There are prettier girls, stronger boys, and smarter kids. It happens. And it will keep happening. Your child will try his hardest and someone else will run faster at the track meet, or get a better test score, or be elected class president. That's a promise.

And what do you say? I wish my son were a faster runner? I wish my daughter were getting straight As?

Naw. You step back and remember that the two of you created a life, and that you have the remarkable privilege of watching and helping it grow. That's why you love your child.

Besides, I don't think that other kid is so cute.

WHAT IS THE SOUND OF
ONE MOUTH FLAPPING?

One of the greatest baby-related inventions of recent times—better than the battery-operated indoor swing but not as sensational as the small, fold-up stroller—is the baby monitor.

You probably already have one of these small transmitters that broadcast a signal from the nursery to a receiver. With it you never have to worry that you haven't heard the baby when he wakes up in the middle of the night or has some scary problem (what if a hawk flew in through the window?) during a nap.

It is a comfort, really, a wonderful invention. However, there is this little drawback: the monitor picks up everything. And when you are, for instance, having a small party at your house, and you and a friend go in to check on the future starting point guard for Stanford, and you take the opportunity to do a little critical evaluation of your guests—"Whoa, has she gained some weight, or what? Who helped stuff her into that skirt?"—they can hear everything.

When that sudden, queasy realization hits you, and you know those words have been broadcast into the ozone, there is only one thing you can do. Stay in that room until everyone has gone home. Because your guests will forget this ever happened eventually—about the time your child enters high school.

THE ART OF
SERENITY AND THE SITTER

Everyone chuckles about how a mom won't let anyone else take care of the baby, but as the weekends begin to pile up without a dinner out, or a movie, or even the annually disappointing office Christmas party, it becomes clear that something must be done. A babysitter must be found.

There are a few simple rules. One: older is better than younger. High school girls mean well but even the most responsible of them often suffer from the opposite of attention deficit disorder. Once focused on something, like a TV movie, video game, or cell phone call, they wouldn't notice if fireballs exploded in the living room.

Two: have prospective sitters meet the baby. If they talk to him, award them one point. If they reach for him, tickle his tummy, and make him smile, they get three points. If they immediately pick him up as if it is the most natural gesture in the world, they get five points.

Three: once you've made your choice—and you have shouted out the last instructions as you are being pushed out the door—stop calling home to see if everything is all right. It is. If it weren't, the sitter would call.

Quit being such a baby.

LEARNING THE
TRUE MANTRA OF BABY TALK

Here's a bulletin. Babies don't talk baby talk. They don't understand baby talk. And when you refer to anyone—whether an infant or a motorcycle policeman—as an "itsoo-bitsoo widdle man," you sound like a nitwit.

It is impossible to stop baby talk. You can only hope to control it. Often it comes from the person you would least expect. One moment your father is explaining the president's economic plan and the next he is asking, "Is this my snuggle-wuggy? Yes, it is. My snuggle-wuggy."

Grandmothers, needless to say, are exempt. Clearly, they cannot help themselves. There is apparently a recessive baby-talk gene that is activated by the birth of a grandchild.

But if you are not a grandmother, did you ever think you might be scaring the poor kid a little? She hears you talking normally all around the house, but suddenly you loom over her and your voice goes all squiggly and strange. Whoa, she wonders, is Dad having a seizure?

A better idea for when you and the baby are sharing a moment? Say, in a normal tone of voice, "You know the problem with the president's economic plan? It is tax based." And tickle her a little so she giggles.

This accomplishes two things. It helps reinforce the baby's recognition of the sound of your voice. And it teaches her to laugh at the president.

THE NOBLE
TRUTH OF DIRT

It is a dirty world out there.

For a long time your baby has been safely swaddled in a spotless blankie covering a clean, fuzzy nightie just out of the dryer. The crib was enveloped with the refreshing aroma of baby powder and lemon-scented diaper wipes.

So it is a bit of a shock to see the face of the future president of the United States smeared with yuck-green creamed peas, hair sticking up in chocolate-pudding spikes.

All part of the new reality. Once the baby gets out of the crib and onto the floor, he has officially moved from the World of Fluffiness to a Life of Grime. Go with it.

Moms, of course, will fight this. Do not let them change the baby's outfits halfway through dinner because a glop of mashed banana has missed the bib. Do not allow them to run for a wet wipe because the dog licked the baby's mouth. It's just a few germs. Everyone will be fine.

The test comes the day you take the baby to the store. Having carefully buckled the baby into his car seat and unloaded the shopping bags into the trunk, you open your car door and, with a huge sigh of relief, flop into the driver's seat. And just as you are ready to leave, the baby power-spits his binkie onto the floor. You have two choices: (a) get out of the car to find a drinking fountain to rinse off the rubber nipple, or (b) brush it off with your hand and put it back in his mouth. What do you do?

That's right, b. Welcome to fatherhood.

BE HERE NOW

Here's a familiar image. A father is sitting in his favorite chair, watching the game on TV. A small child is tugging at his arm.

"Dad? Hey, Dad?" he says. "Watch this. Look."

What the future Wimbledon tennis champion doesn't realize, of course, is that the ball is on the 23, the clock is winding down, and if the offense doesn't get a first down on this play the whole game will be over. Are you watching your child? Sure. Sort of.

So when she says, "Did you see it, Dad?" and you look over and realize you missed it, you probably feel a stab of remorse, wondering if you are a bad dad.

You are.

Just like the rest of us.

There's a famous story about two Zen monks who are raving about their respective teachers. One says his teacher is remarkable. He can write in the air on one side of the river and the letters appear on a page on the other side.

The other says his teacher is even greater. "When he eats he does nothing but eat. When he drinks he does nothing but drink. When he sleeps he does nothing but sleep."

Hearing this, the first monk bows to the greater feat. And he's right. It isn't easy. But it is worth pursuing.

Be here now.

THE DHARMA OF **TWO** A.M.

You may have already learned to interpret the crying. There's the high-pitched squawl when a finger gets pinched and the angry, uncomfortable wail that says, "Helloooooo? We need a diaper check over here!"

And there is that weary, forlorn whine that says, "Honestly-I-don't-really-need-anything,-but-I-am-worn-out-and-cranky-and-I-am-not-going-to-sleep-until-I-can't-keep-my-eyes-open-any-longer." This is not a big deal if it happens around the usual noon nap. However, at two in the morning, with both parents expected at work early the next morning, crabby crying is no fun.

There are several ways to deal with this. Some parents end up moving the baby into their bed. Some roll the crib into the bedroom in order to monitor every hiccup.

And that's just fine. We are not here to judge. But wouldn't it be nice to have your own space, a snug and comfy refuge for the night? Because sooner or later, the future delegate to the United Nations is going to have to sleep on his own. Certainly by the time he is sixteen or seventeen.

So, and it pains us to tell you this, you are going to have to let the baby cry. You have to go in, check the diaper dipstick, make sure the blankets and pajamas are in place, whisper a reassuring "night-night," and leave.

There will be a surprised yowl when you go, followed by some really angry bellowing, which will subside into a tired, cranky whimper. And then, miraculously, he will fall asleep.

The whole process usually takes only about fifteen minutes—and less and less as it becomes a nightly routine. And for the two of you, lying in bed, gritting your teeth, and doing nothing while your wonderful child weeps, it won't seem like more than four or five hours.

BE THE TOY

As the future world-renowned architect begins to get up and move around the house, toys will become a major focus. In an odd way this is—stick with me here—like dog food.

As we know, dog and food companies aren't trying to create a product that pets will like. They are marketing to *you*. That's why they make puppy treats shaped like fire hydrants. Because (hello?) a dog doesn't know that's funny.

Toddler toy marketing can be like that. Is the toy something the kid would like—interactive, noisy, and colorful? Or is it an adult's idea of what the perfect child should own—educational, politically correct, and . . . did we already say "educational"?

Remember hearing about buying an expensive toy and the kid ends up playing with the box? That's not a joke. You wouldn't think you'd fall for a $400 "Learn the State Capitals!" fun pack, but the danger is there. The lesson? Don't buy expensive, fragile toys. They break. People get mad. Hurt feelings ensue.

Toys should be sturdy but soft, making no more noise than a little jingle or soft rattle sound. Cows that moo, chickens that cluck, and dogs that bark will eventually drive you straight up the wall.

Jack-in-the-boxes are both scary and annoying, but activity centers—where you push a button, turn a handle, or flip a lever to make something pop up—can be a blast. Want the test? Sometimes, sitting by yourself with the activity center within reach, do you lean over and poke the big red button to make the clown pop out of the window?

You'd never do that? Right. Hold that thought and get back to us.

CHAOS THEORY
AND THE LITTLE RED WAGON

For a long time the vehicles of choice for little kids were the tricycle and the little red wagon (LRW). Or, as they were known at the pediatrician's office, guaranteed full-time employment.

Whoever had the idea to sit a toddler on a three-wheeled trike, high above the sidewalk, must have owned stock in the plaster cast industry. Old-fashioned trikes were the perfect mechanism to cause broken arms, head bumps, and skinned elbows. No wonder they have all but disappeared.

Little red wagons are sneakier. They look cute and somewhere it is written that every kid should have one. Grandparents, in particular, seem to find the mystical attraction of the LRW irresistible and can't wait to bring one over.

You need to stop them. The LRW seems harmless, but that is only until the wheels are turned all the way in one direction, the future Daytona 500 NASCAR champion leans the other way, and the whole thing tips over in an eyeblink. Not to mention the injuries that can happen when she gets a little older, jumps in the LRW, coasts down the driveway, and careens out into the street in this vehicle with no brakes and minimal steering.

Skip the trike and the LRW and go for one of those pedal-powered "big wheels." They are stable and close to the ground and they can be stopped by holding down the pedals. Unfortunately, they have hard plastic wheels that, on a concrete sidewalk, sound something like a cross between a bowling ball rolling through a rain culvert and a jet airliner taking off.

But it's either that or the wail of someone who has just been spilled onto the sidewalk. Your call.

THE INNER DIALOGUE

There is absolutely nothing wrong with keeping up a steady stream of chatter when you and the future chairman of the World Bank are out for a walk. Of course, if you saw a transcript of your conversation you might wonder if you'd undergone a lobotomy.

"Is that a doggie? Yes it is. Doggie goes woof! Woof, woof!"

It's all part of developing those language skills, familiarizing baby with daddy's speech patterns, and matching physical objects with abstract verbal cues. Perfectly acceptable and even encouraged.

But you might also find yourself falling into a kind of free association commentary on the world around you while, say, strolling the aisles at the supermarket.

"Did Mommy say to get endive or rosemary? Whoa, three fifty a bunch? Does Mommy think Daddy has won the lottery?"

You'll want to keep an eye on that. Not because you'll say anything embarrassing or that folks will find it odd. Anyone talking to a baby gets to say whatever he wants.

No, the real problem is that your license to talk to yourself may be revoked if you don't watch it. Your little discussion partner might nod off in the comfy stroller seat without your knowledge.

This changes everything.

Because one minute you are teaching your child critical language skills. And the next you are just some nut talking to himself in public.

THE ZEN OF THE BINKIE

You may encounter controversies over diapers (cloth or disposable?). Over feeding (breast or bottle?). And definitely over potty training (sooner or later?).

But nothing beats the binkie controversy.

The binkie, as you know, is a pacifier, a rubber nipple with a plastic handle. When it is not time to eat and the future Academy Award–winning actress is fussy, you can pop a binkie in her mouth and suddenly the crying gives way to the soft, contented squeak of synthetic nursing. Unfortunately, the plastic mouth guard gives your child the look of Hannibal Lecter, but would you rather hear cranky wailing?

Apparently some people would. The binkie may not look like it, but it is actually a free pass for busybodies who want to tell you that your baby is (a) much too old to have a binkie, or (b) going to get such severe buckteeth that she will be able to eat corn through a picket fence.

There are several possible responses to these comments, one or two of which can be printed. Look, if they really wanted to help they could change a diaper.

Binkies have been in use for centuries—well, decades, anyhow—and everyone seems to have turned out all right. They make the baby happy, and you too. First, take a deep, cleansing breath and find your *hara*, or center.

Then tell the binkie police to mind their own beeswax.

BUDDHA
AND THE BREAST

When the baby arrives there may be some thought of breast-feeding. This is an excellent idea—healthy, natural, and comforting.

It can also provide inspiration for many hilarious quips from the parent who does not have breasts. Some of these witticisms are simply too amusing to keep to oneself and you will want to share them with your partner for a much-needed laugh.

Do not, under any circumstances, do that.

Remember the snippy correction we were given when we blithely told the wives of friends that "we" were in labor? This is another one of those. References to the increased size of the breasts (especially using the phrase "whoo-hoo"), to "meals on heels," or to how you wish you could get up for the 3:00 A.M. feeding but "don't have the equipment" will not be appreciated.

In addition, if, through some monumental lapse of common sense, you should ever lightheartedly make any reference whatsoever to the word "cow," you may be killed. And just so we are clear—there is not a jury of women in the world who would not let your wife off on grounds of justifiable homicide.

TAI CHI CHUAN
WHEN TOTING A BABY

To be blunt, a toddler can be a load.

In theory, infants are adorable little bundles of fluff floating in your arms. But once they get a little older, especially by the time they ride on your hip with an arm hooked around your neck, it is not unfair to make a comparison to a sack of cement.

There are several solutions to this problem. Our Zen friends would think in terms of tai chi chuan, or movements to maximize the flow of energy. The key is to find a way to hold and carry a squirming energy ball. However, you should be warned: not all baby totes are created equal.

There is the front loader, which leaves the future secretary of state suspended on your chest, facing forward, blinking, with legs and arms dangling. This is fine, although it may appear that a large starfish has been superglued to your sternum.

For a long time the carrier of choice was the papoose-style backpack, which was both comfortable and convenient. However, it was hard to see what was going on back there, and when baby dozed off, the sight of his head lolling awkwardly would give some passersby a start.

The fact is that the best method is probably the oldest. Pick him up, set him on your hip, and hold on. He'll be walking around soon enough.

KENSHO:
A MOMENT OF ENLIGHTENMENT

How many people in the last six months have felt it necessary to inform you ominously that having a baby is "going to change your life"? A lot, right?

They can't help themselves.

Let's get this straight. Of course it is going to change your life. So would switching jobs, buying a motorcycle, or deciding to become a Buddhist monk. Every change in life changes your life.

But you won't suddenly begin speaking French or raising orchids. With a baby in the house there is less sleep, more crying, and fewer beers with the boys. Isn't that pretty much how you had it figured?

People who pull you aside, look deep into your eyes, and warn you that having a baby will change your life are doing one of two things. Either they don't get the dad thing. Or they are worried about what will happen to themselves when they become dads.

Ignore them.

NIRVANA AND THE
HORNS OF SHAMPOO

A bath sounds like a lot more trouble than it really is. When you and the baby's mom have settled down on the couch and that mindless but entertaining TV show has just started, giving a bath doesn't sound very appealing. But someone has to get up and give the future commander of the Mars space probe a scrub. And sometimes it should be you.

You should, of course, whine a little before volunteering, just to make certain that your bonus points are being recorded. Then you can scoop up the bathee, start the water, and begin gathering the obligatory bushel basket of aquatic toys.

Just to be clear, the bath is not about getting clean. The bath is about sliding, splashing, and giggling. There will be some water outside the exact bathing area, so let's just quit worrying about that. Duckies will make high dives, boats will be sunk, and toy squirting will take place.

Naturally, soap must be applied at some point, which makes things even more slippery, leading to more sliding, splashing, and giggling. Hair must be washed (with "no tears" soap, of course), and that leads to the transcendent moment of being the father of a child of a certain age—shampoo horns.

You will definitely want to create shampoo horns, the bigger and gaudier the better. Whip the frothy shampoo-covered hair into as wild and complicated a shape as possible. Then find a mirror, show the shampoo hornee, and set aside time for uncontrollable hee-hawing. Then, and this is important, take a picture.

Because when you two get out, and mom looks into the bathroom with horror, and screams, "This place is soaked!" the two of you can exchange a look.

We know.

And you'll want a photo to help you remember that.

THE
COSMIC STEP FORWARD

Up until now the baby's self-propulsion has been limited. He may have done some crawling—or even a lot of crawling—but you can't get much safer than creeping around on all fours.

However, at some point you are going to look down and see the future *New York Times* best-selling author teetering on two feet, holding a chair or low table, and preparing to take a step. At this point all bets are off.

There is nothing that prepares you for life as a dad like watching your offspring learn to walk. It is exhilarating, scary, and unavoidable.

Let's begin with some harsh realities. There will be falls. There will be crying. When your little drunken sailor sets off on a jaunt, bruises are likely and at some point a skinned knee will be almost a sure thing. As he wobbles forward, careens sideways, and lurches backwards, you will see danger everywhere: the bricks in the fireplace, the sharp edge of the end table, and the slick floor where the rug doesn't cover it.

What you need to do in those cases is notice how eager he is to get back up and try it again—even after a bad bump. What you may find is that once he gets the hang of it, he will deliberately walk away from you, off on his own. Your job is to stand to the side, hold out a hand if needed, and offer encouragement.

It isn't easy at times, but get used to it. That's pretty much your job description for the next eighteen to twenty years.

THE MIGHTY VIRTUE OF A
DAUGHTER AND A DAD

Deep in the secret depths of their silent hearts, some fathers are the tiniest bit disappointed when they learn the new baby will be a girl.

This is an epic error. For starters, girls play sports now. A lot. And these aren't bunt-and-giggle games either. Elbows are thrown, knees are skinned, and trash is talked.

But that's not really the point. Explaining the mysterious, powerful bond between dads and daughters takes a lifetime. Why is it that you two can speak without saying a word? Or can sense each other's moods? Does her mom complain that you sometimes let her get away with murder?

Um . . . maybe. Is that a problem?

A daughter will unexpectedly give you a hug. Or sit with you and watch your favorite classic movie on TV.

In fact, you are likely to find that your daughter is a nearly perfect companion. She likes and understands you. Which is why, when she goes on a date, you may find your heart taking an unexpected lurch. Remember when you secretly wished she was a boy? This is payback.

THE MIGHTY VIRTUE OF
A SON AND A DAD

Every dad wants a son. And that's where the problems start. Hopefully you haven't named him after yourself. That's a red flag even a complete stranger can't miss.

It's silly, really. If you met someone new in everyday life you wouldn't dream of suggesting that he start dressing like you, or develop the same interests, or believe what you believe.

Your son is that person. He's someone new in your life. And there is no telling what he will be like. The sons of wonky computer geeks sometimes become football players. There are vegetarians whose male child has turned out to be a duck hunter.

Now, you say you wish you could see yourself in your son? Oh, you'll see yourself all right. Your temper, your impatience with small bolts and tiny nuts, your lack of dazzling speed on the playing field.

Too often dads like to think that their son is going to embody everything good about them, except a little bit better. Actually, your son is much more likely to get the whole package, warts and all. (Warts are hereditary, by the way.) The good news? The two of you can work on those warts together.

SERENITY,
SIMPLICITY,
⬤ AND THE STROLLER ⬤

There is, right this second, a space-age baby stroller about to go into production. There always is.

Wait until you see it. It will have adjustable snap grommets, full-range wheel rotation, and an ergonomic (and educational) backrest for the baby. It will be *the* infant accessory this year.

You don't need it.

Baby strollers exist in two realities. The first is the catalog and the showroom. The second is the real world, in which you must attempt to maneuver a rolling bathtub between the tables at a crowded restaurant. And in which reality are we going to spend most of our time?

You need a stroller that is light, comfy, and—this is important—easy to fold. The small, collapsible umbrella version is perfectly fine.

It folds down in a jiffy, it can be slipped under the table when you're out to eat, and if it gets swiped or broken, who cares? It didn't cost much more than a box of diapers. If you want to go all out, get one with a sun shade.

Oh, and if you see other parents pushing one of those British perambulators that look like a Humvee with handles?

Hold the door for them. They could use the help.

THE
COSMIC DIAPER:
A MEDITATION

There was a time when babies wore cloth diapers. Some still do, and bless their parents for saving the ozone. But the vast majority of baby bottoms are now covered with throwaway diapers with tape on the sides.

No more painful pokes with the points of safety pins. No more toting a bag of loaded diapers whose fumes would set off a department-store fire alarm. Big improvements.

However . . .

There are a few quirks. While a good Buddhist might believe that there are endless opportunities for reincarnation, the tape only works once, for example. If you mis-diaper—say putting it on backwards—you will not be able to reseal the package. Also, there is a saturation point for paper diapers. In the case of a diaper shortage, if you attempt to stretch the life of the disposable, you may find that it tends to, well, disintegrate.

Actually, that can be a good thing. Because if diapers weren't such a mess, you'd never be pushed to attempt one of life's most maddening and difficult tasks—potty training.

FIND
YOUR SENSEI

If there were one tidbit of advice we'd want new fathers to take away, it would be this: watch the veterans and choose a *sensei*, or mentor. Pick out a family with more than one child, a family that seems to have it together, and keep an eye on the parents. What you are likely to find is that they are not rushing to the front at the Christmas play, elbowing others out of the way so they can get the best angle for their videocamera.

Instead, you will probably find them in the back, looking relaxed and in control. And afterward, they don't make a fuss, even when their future shortstop for the Giants gets the big hit that wins it all for the Pee-Wee League Marauders. They tell their son or daughter that they are proud but they also direct some attention to others. Their approach provides a good lesson for the child, but a better one for rookie dads and moms.

Because a lot of first-time parents worry about how they are doing. They think people are watching them and judging their actions with their children.

That's just silly.

People don't judge parents by how they act with their kids. They judge them by how their kids act later. It might be worthwhile to keep that in mind.

THE TAO (THE WAY) OF DREAMLAND

Let's say it is the middle of the night. You're bleary eyed, your wife has already gone back to bed (sorry, it's your night), and even the future international bond trader is yawning. But despite your best efforts—walking the floor while humming softly, bouncing gently—nothing.

At this point there is only one thing to do. Get in the car.

No, not to drive away and check into a motel. You need to take the baby for a ride. There is nothing like the vibration of a moving car to put a fussy baby to sleep. It worked so well for us that for a while we were afraid we had a leak in our exhaust pipe.

Now, you may balk at the idea of cruising the streets in your pajamas—at least on a regular basis—and that's fine.

In that case we mention the clothes dryer. Placing the baby in a child seat, putting her atop the dryer, and starting it up supplies that same steady, soothing vibration. The little fussbudget nods off and can be put to bed. (Obviously, you'd stay right there during the process. No matter how sleep deprived you are, I know you wouldn't think of leaving your baby, even for a second, on a running clothes dryer.)

Now, would I ever recommend placing your baby on a large household appliance and starting it up just to get some sleep?

Absolutely not.

I am just saying it has been done. And it works.

BECOMING ONE WITH YOUR SCALE

Pregnancy is all about getting bigger. Unfortunately, you probably thought that only applied to the preg-nee. Or, to put it another way, mom is eating for two—what's your excuse?

There is no time in a woman's life when she feels less guilt about indulging herself than when she is carrying a child. Which is perfectly understandable. At our house we used to keep a decadent, gooey dessert, and a *backup* decadent, gooey dessert, in the fridge at all times.

Weight will be gained. That's a given. Some of it—probably more than you expected—will be yours.

Before, if this happened, you would immediately throw yourself into an intensive, full-body exercise program with a strict, New Age diet plan. And that is an excellent idea. Unfortunately, you have zero chance of making that happen. There's no one to watch the baby while you take off for a four-mile run or an hour at the gym. And as far as food goes, you're just lucky to get some. Pipe down and eat.

THE GREAT LEAP — OR SLIDE

Going down the slide is a concept, not an event. It embraces the complex push-pull of fatherhood. We are delighted when the future Olympic gold medalist in gymnastics tries something new and adventurous, but there's a side of us that sees nothing but pointy corners, slippery floors, and potholes in footpaths. You have to let that go.

In our family it all happened at the playground. My daughter, a legendary daredevil who would turn into a skateboarder, boogie boarder, and all-around jock, wanted to go down the slide. By herself.

This was not a huge problem. She'd done the slide before, with help, and despite the fretting and arm waving we were sure she could climb the ladder. But she did look awfully small and young when she reached the top of the high, curving, scary slide.

As she perched up there, a hush fell over the playground. Other parents did the tennis-match head swivel—looking at us, then at our daughter, then back at us. We got it. They disapproved.

After a long, long pause our little darling pushed off, and flipped off the first turn and crashed smack on her face. Not only was she bawling her head off but she'd also split her lip, so there was blood, just to confirm that we were irresponsible nitwits.

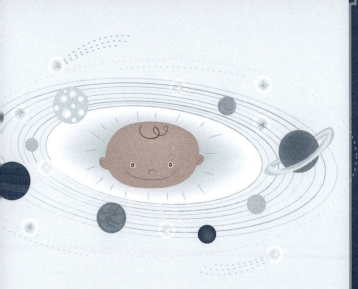

The cleanup took quite a while, long enough for the other parents to leave the playground, some muttering under their breath.

Which is when my daughter got up, climbed the ladder again, and came down the slide without so much as a wobble. Hey, it was something she wanted to do. All we could do was stand back and watch—with a tissue ready.

THE INNER NAME

It will not be long before you find yourself referring to the baby by one of several adorable nicknames. Snickerdoodle, Sparky, Buzz, Boo-Boo, Bumbie, Pumpkin Pie—everyone does it. And it is charming.

Just a word of caution. Cute pet names are incredibly slippery, and later in life one may accidentally slide out of your mouth at a time that little Boopsie may not find appropriate (for example, when meeting her date for the Homecoming Dance).

Just something to keep in mind when you begin lightheartedly referring to your newborn as "Stinky."

GO WITH THE **FLU FLOW**

Mom has disinfected every surface
with alcohol wipes. She's required
anyone who wants to hold the baby
to have his or her hands steam
cleaned. Bottles and nipples have
been boiled until they are nearly
melting into a puddle of rubber
and plastic.

And the future host of the
Tonight Show still gets sick.

It is at this point that you learn
an important lesson. When the baby
is ill everyone feels lousy. Babies do
not shrug off sore throats or runny
noses, or wave off sympathy and say, "Oh, it is just a little
headache; If I just rest for a moment, I am sure it will be gone
in a jiffy."

Babies settle into sickness the way we all did before
someone taught us to be good soldiers or brave buckeroos.
They may cry, softly but miserably, for hours. You may, for
the first time, understand what someone means when they
say their baby has "sick eyes."

The solution when you're on sick watch? Surrender to
the germ. Stay in those morning sweatpants. Plan the day
around sniffling and cranky crying. And drink plenty of fluids.

Because—oh, yeah—you're going to get it next.

Guaranteed.

FOOD, WAITERS,
AND THE GREATER TRUTH

It is not as if you can't find a sitter. Or that you don't want to leave the baby with anyone. (That's just ridiculous. It just so happens that no good opportunities for a night out have come up in the last twelve consecutive weekends.)

But there are times when you want to get out of the house and actually sit down in a restaurant for a meal. Believe it or not, sometimes it makes more sense to take the little cracker muncher with you. Nothing could be simpler.

First, be sure you've laid in a selection of treats and toys to keep the future pastry chef at Le Cirque quiet and fascinated. (Do not, however, make the rookie mistake of handing them out too quickly, or, worse yet, all at once. Dole them out carefully, saving the big, messy treat for last.)

That said, you'll want to move right along once you reach the eatery. This is a business trip, not a vacation. Order everything at once and eat with one hand while amusing the baby with the other. Keep things rolling.

On the other hand, you may find that you have never had such fast service in your life. There is likely to be no shilly-shallying or dilly-dallying. In one memorable meal in our family history, a waiter attempted to bring us our salad, main course, and check all at the same time.

You are likely to be seated, fed, and back out the door in nothing flat. You will end up on the sidewalk both pleased with the experience and slightly dazed.

Kind of reminds you of the whole fatherhood thing, doesn't it?

THE IMAGE AND REALITY

There are two kinds of new parents: ones who record every single waking moment of their child's life and those who are constantly slapping their foreheads and saying, "I wish we had the camera."

Sometimes they are the same people.

The future runway model for Versace will react to the clicking shutters and whirring videocamera in a steady progression of behavior: oblivious, cooperative, and finally the infant equivalent of "Guys, can we give it a break?"

And she has a point.

Look, there are some irresistibly cute moments. Somehow you will catch a few of them and they will become a part of the family lore. Years from now you will look at that image, nudge your partner, and smile—guaranteed.

But there's a lot of junk too. Blurred shots from when the baby moved at the last minute. Horrible, embarrassing scenes of your partner with puffy eyes, rooster-tail hair, and ratty sweatpants after spending all night trying to calm a crying baby. And you—put a shirt on, would you?

Trust us. Nobody wants to see that. Not your friends, not your family, and, once you come to your senses, not you. When your child takes that first step, do you want her to look up and see your face or a flashbulb?

Relax. Step away from the camera. There's some real life taking place here.

SESSHIN: INTENSE TRAINING
(IN THIS CASE FOR THE POTTY)

At some point the simple pleasure and novelty of unwrapping a wet and stinky diaper wears off. During the process, you look down at the future leading scorer for the World Cup soccer team and realize that this is bliss for him. He makes a mess; you clean it up—with lemon-fresh wipes and a dash of scented powder, too. He doesn't care if things ever change.

So, inevitably, you think about potty training. After all, Mary Lou Johnson's kid, down the street, is not only using the toilet but he can also play the first few bars of "Eine Kleine Nachtmusik," on the piano.

And this is a good time to make some points about those two household appliances—the piano and the toilet. Each takes plenty of practice, requires a seated position, and the results generally stink. Oh, and one more thing, a child shouldn't be shoved in their direction until they show some interest.

Because there is really only one problem with the baby books that suggest you put a child on the potty at nine months and twelve days.

It doesn't work.

Expressing disappointment when there is an "accident," praising others who wear "big boy underwear," or wishing aloud that your child would act more "grown-up" is a mistake. Until now, as far as he knew, you loved everything about him.

Now it sounds as if you are having second thoughts.

Look, in the history of indoor plumbing have you ever heard of a kid who was unable to be potty trained? No, you have not. Relax and show a little patience.

And hope he'll do the same for you someday when you're in the rest home and having the same problem.

INNER KNOWLEDGE AND DR. SEUSS

When the future Grand Prix championship driver gets older and you look back on these years you are bound to have some regrets. Odd little moments that stick in your mind, those times when you were too tired, or distracted, or—let's just say it—selfish.

The funny thing is, most of them probably bother you a lot more than they bother anyone else.

"I have always felt bad about the time when you wanted to come to the city with me and I told you I was too busy," you may confess later. "I will never forget how you cried and cried."

"Really?" your child will probably say. *"When was that again?"*

But there is one regret that never goes away—missing a chance to tuck her in at night. It is the easiest thing in the world to skip. You're tired, there's a show on TV, and you have hardly spent any time with your wife. You just need a little time to unwind.

And you deserve it. Right after you sit on the side of the bed, open a book, and read something out loud. Sometimes you don't even get to the reading, because of the recap of important events that took place at the park. And sometimes, let's be honest, it is hard to get a child to even pay attention.

But mostly it works. Sometimes you do the funny voices and sometimes you forget (or try to skip them) and have to be reminded. A lot of times you end up reading the same story over and over and over.

But just a word of advice. It won't be so long before you will walk by that room and that bed will be empty. You'll wish a lot of things. But one of them will not be that you missed a night or two discussing the significance of *Green Eggs and Ham*.

EMBRACE
THE DIVERSITY

Here's some advice you probably won't accept. And that's all right. No one does.

It is possible that this is your second child. Or third. Or fifth. Who knows? The point is that you will want to use what you have learned while raising the previous child to mentor and raise your next.

Don't do that.

OK, some of it is fine. The proper operation of a diaper, formula mixing tips, and stroller management are all helpful skills. But if there is one point you need to hear (and people are going to tell you even if you don't listen) it is this: every child is different.

We're not talking freckles or no freckles here. We mean vastly, dramatically, whole other personality different. So different that much of what you have already learned is useless. All you can do is sit back, remain patient, and wait to see what you've got.

At our house we took our son out to the backyard with a ball and glove as soon as he was old enough to stand and catch. He was bored stiff. No interest in playing catch. So when our daughter came along we didn't even bother. And she ended up meeting us at the door every evening with two gloves and a ball, begging to play.

Different. Who knew?

FIRST DAY AT THE ZENDO

Needless to say, there is one thing you must never do. You should not, under any circumstances, send your child to one of those kiddie day-care facilities. First, they are hothouses for diseases, bad behavior, and pointy objects. Second, as everyone knows, the moment you drop your child off, she'll experience feelings of abandonment and loss that will never, ever be overcome.

Just kidding.

Of course you are going to send the future CEO of Amalgamated Microsystems to day care, just as the Buddhist monk must make his way to the *zendo*, or meeting hall. How else is she going to play with other kids, learn shocking new words, and—hey, it has to happen some day—take those first steps away from you?

Now, it is possible that there was once a child who walked through the doors on her first day, gave her parents a quick kiss, and dashed off happily to meet new friends. Trust us—that is not your child. Or anyone else's we know.

There will be clinging. There will be crying. And there may be one of those awful scenes where your little darling, screaming at the top of her lungs, is peeled out of your arms by the nice day-care lady, who is saying something like, "We are going to have FUN! Don't you want to have FUN?"

However, if you stick with this it will work. But you must be resolute. You cannot, under any circumstances, cave in and say, "All right, let's go home and try this again tomorrow." The child should get the impression that this is the new routine, it takes place every day, and that is that.

Now, there will probably be times when you feel like a bigger heel than the moment when you walk out the door as your child wails and calls your name. But none comes to mind. It isn't easy.

But some day-care facilities actually let you try this strategy: You go out the door, wait about ten minutes, and then creep around to the side and peek in through a window. What you are likely to see is your little emotional basket case, tears still on her cheeks, playing with a new toy.

In fact, it doesn't look as if she misses you much at all.

SPORTS AND WU WEI

Sports are a healthy, enjoyable, and fun way to learn self-confidence, self-reliance, and physical skills.

Right. And you're the Chancellor of the Exchequer.

The fact is that sports can be all of those things. But they take a wise and strenuous effort. There is nothing that causes more upset, tears, and hurt feelings between parents (often just dads) and their children than simple Saturday afternoon games/meets/matches.

Can I just make this plea right now? Let the kid play the sports he wants. Or none, if that's his choice. If crying ensues, something is wrong. If you have raised your voice to criticize, complain, or express disappointment in your child's play, something is wrong. The Zen concept is *wu wei*, the nonforcing way. Keep reminding yourself of that.

But that's all for later, a few years from now. For now the future soloist for the New York City Ballet (hey, you never know; and if that's his choice keep your yap shut and support him) is just trying to learn to take three consecutive steps. No pressure.

Except sometimes there kind of is. How often do you see a kid decked out in game gear from his dad's favorite team? And it is sorta cute, isn't it?

Yeah, every once in a while. But if this is the dress code day after day, outfit after outfit, somebody is missing the point. Buying the $200 toddler-sized version of Michael Jordan shoes isn't adorable; it is the beginning of a cultural choice that says you are not valued unless you are a superstar athlete. What you wear is a big part of who you are when you are a kid.

Let him make the choice. If he wants football jerseys and basketball shorts, fine. He will let you know. Stop projecting. If you think sports gear is cool, wear it yourself.

Although, honestly, I have to tell you—you're getting a little old for that stuff.

KINHIN:
WALKING MEDITATION

As the future chief scientist for MIT's research team gets a little older and a little more mobile, you may be surprised at how much you enjoy going for a walk. Strolling around the block or taking a leisurely meander over to the neighborhood park may never have struck you as a terrific idea for a Sunday afternoon, but now you may find yourself looking forward to it.

On one hand it is kind of funny because the baby could probably take it or leave it. Not that she doesn't enjoy a jaunt. It's fine, really. But a good part of the time she may just fall asleep, her little knitted cap nodding off to the side as she snoozes away in the stroller seat.

You, however, may find it to be your first-choice fallback activity when things get a little slow on the weekend. Halftime during football game is a nearly perfect time—especially if it is starting to look as if there might be a suggestion of cleaning out the garage on the horizon.

But this isn't just about ducking chores. It really is enjoy-able. You can take your time, check out the new sprinkler system in your neighbor's front yard, or look over the new car in the driveway down the street.

Frankly, if you were doing this by yourself, people would wonder what you were up to. But you've got a baby. You get a free pass.

THE PERFECT VIRTUE OF A ROMPER

Cute does not begin to describe the range of toddler-sized supermodel outfits on the market. There are precious pinafore dresses (with plenty of petticoats), miniature designer jeans, and teeny Hawaiian shirts with board shorts.

There was even a brief fad involving little white fur coats for girls. Thankfully, that didn't last long. They looked like the result of some horrible experiment with the family poodle.

Now, let's give you a little credit. You are not going to dress the future chairman of the Ways and Means Committee in a tiny tuxedo. You are already aware that hardly any little girls actually wear those frilly dresses, the ones that end up getting passed from family to family without ever being seen on a child.

However, many parents do have a tendency—well intentioned but misguided—to go for the "well turned out" look. Here we are basically talking miniature versions of grown-up fashions—matching tops and pants, skirts and sweaters, and, most of all, adorable, whimsical hats.

The problems quickly become apparent. First, kids hate hats. Second, buttons. Getting them fastened takes forever, and keeping them hooked, while an engrossing hobby, can eat up hours of the day. Dresses, while making a child look very grown-up, take a concentrated effort to keep in place. And frankly, most toddler girls are likely to hoist their skirts up at odd moments to get at a particularly vexing itch.

Not that anyone is going to be scandalized by the sight of a diaper. This isn't a visit from the etiquette police. It is just that often little kids in grown-up outfits look phony, contrived, and (most of all) uncomfortable.

Take a step back and consider. When do things work best? When you are tugging down the designer sweater in order to cover your son's tummy (again)? Or when he is zipped into a comfy full-length romper, preferably with feet?

You know the answer. The one-piece fleece is comfy, practical, and without fuss. If mom wants to turn your toddler into a runway model, let her—when she is taking care of her. When you have her, go with what we like to call "the all day-er." Perfect for any occasion—at least until she's thirteen or fourteen.

THE JOURNEY AND THE DESTINATION

It is one thing to put the future Air Force test pilot in a buggy and push him in a brisk, efficient trip down the sidewalk. It is another to set those little feet free and let them wander. Still tippy—having barely learned to balance in those two tiny shoes—the little explorer charts an odd, haphazard course down the street.

There will probably be pointing, at random flowers or stray kitties. And perhaps some grand gestures, sweeps of the arm that imply visions and thoughts that are larger than mere words. Surely he will attempt to push the stroller, generally directly into a tree or off the curb and into the street.

And that's fine. But you are not, are you? It is entirely possible to have embarked fifteen or twenty minutes ago and still be in sight of your front door. If you could just reach down and straighten out the path of the stroller, for example, you could make much better time.

Go ahead. Give it a try. Say, "C'mon, let's go," and give a gentle tug to Magellan's hand. Or nudge the stroller toward the park. See what happens.

The squawk will begin almost immediately. He may yank his hand away or even attempt to spin away and run off. Hey, whose walk is this, anyhow?

Wait for it. The answer will dawn on you eventually.

(Hint: It isn't yours.)

LIVE IN THE
MOMENT OF CREAMED CORN

Zen masters say, "Live in the moment of your eating. Experience eating."

Good news. The moment you start to switch your baby from milk to solid food you will definitely begin to "experience eating." But you may not have expected it to be a full-body experience.

You will probably begin with applesauce. Excellent. The future book editor of the *New York Times* will probably happily scarf down a spoonful of applesauce. And, just as a wild guess, the same is likely to happen with pureed peaches, blended bananas, and—to go way out on a limb—pudding.

Wonderful. But baby needs some veggies, right? So between bites of apricot puree and vanilla pudding, you sneak in something like a spoonful of creamed spinach.

The effect will be instantaneous. Eyes closed, lips puckered, and nose scrunched, your child will wear the hilarious expression of someone who has just chugged a glass of lemon extract. Then the broccoli medley or strained beets will shoot out the mouth and all over everything.

This is the beginning of food spitting. Later there will be spoon grabbing and eventually creamed carrot throwing. Oh yeah, you'll be experiencing your food.

And someday, when your baby has grown to be a teenager and you are watching her munch cold french fries for breakfast, you will wonder why it seemed so important to push the concept of green bean surprise.

CROUCHING FATHER, HIDDEN TODDLER

Spying on your child is nothing to brag about. Not that you don't do it, of course. When you come down the hall and hear him chattering to himself in the next room, the urge to sneak up and peak around the corner is genetically irresistible.

The result may surprise you. No, not that your son is using his Happy Time dump truck to run over Clarence the talking brontosaurus. That's going to happen.

But watching him play in happy solitude is bound to trigger a flood of memories, even as young as he is. You know what it is about seeing a baby lost in his own little world that makes fathers so wistful? For a moment at least, he doesn't need you.

You may think back to that crazy, scary, amazing day when he was born. Or the summer evening when he pointed to the big round moon in the sky and said "ball" for the first time. Or the close calls—the time he toppled down the stairs or fell in the swimming pool. Chances are, even at this age, he already has a scar or two, proof that he's bumped up against the rough edges of life. There are more to come.

You may wonder when those reminiscences begin to fade. They don't. Oh, you may not recall the name of his kindergarten teacher in a couple of years, but those secret snapshots create a photo album in your mind. Funny how they always seem to form when he doesn't know you are looking, lost in concentration building an alphabet block fort or shoveling sand into a yellow plastic bucket.

Those are the moments when he has forgotten that you exist. And it is just a little foreshadowing. Pretty soon he will start walking away. The fact is, from the moment he takes his first step he is starting to move away from you. To his classroom for the first day of school, to the car for his first date, and finally, down the sidewalk, to live on his own.

That's how it works. The key is to pay attention, savor those moments, and hold them in your heart.

If you do, it's not a bad trade.

ACKNOWLEDGMENTS

Sincere thanks to editor Lisa Campbell, whose guidance, encouragement, and deft touch with Zen phrases—especially this book's title—made the concept work. To my agent, Joe Spieler, deliberate but steady. And to Chronicle Books' Bill LeBlond, who recommended me for this project despite my sketchy play on the softball field.

C. W. NEVIUS is a former sports columnist who discovered that dealing with coddled and demanding elite athletes was the perfect training for raising two children. He now writes about kids and families, among other things, in the *San Francisco Chronicle*. He lives in Northern California.

BEEGEE TOLPA is a Seattle-based illustrator and graphic designer. Her clients include IBM, Britain's Royal Mail, and numerous magazines.